MARIN LANDSCAPE DESIGN

Dane E. Rose

MARIN LANDSCAPE DESIGN

Illustrations and Layout by Dane E. Rose

Phone: 415 455 9161

daneeaster@comcast.net

www.MysticalLandscapes.com

Published by: www.MarinGardener.org

ISBN-13: 978-1500357351

CONTENTS

This book is dedicated to the

people who taught me what I

know and to the clients who

give me an opportunity to

to share it.

INTRODUCTION

Most of the coffee-table landscape books I've read have impressive photography that can blow this book out of the water. What they don't have are the nuts and bolts needed to make good decisions such as a detailed discussion of costs, permits, parking , couple dynamics and deer. I wanted this book to be different.

This book covers many of the blind spots that are not covered in most landscape books but which affect the function and appearance of your garden. I've included chapters on driveway surfaces, garage doors, mailboxes, retaining walls, fences and gates. I've grouped these by category rather than by garden to make it easy for you to make decisions and discover what you like. My hope is that you will find a picture that is close enough to what you want that you can easily communicate your preference to a partner, landscape designer or contractor.

Good design is not limited to beauty. It benefits your relaxation, resale value, bank account, and the environment. Poorly thought-out ideas are installed all the time and many of them get redone a few years later. This means that money, time, and resources get spent to install, remove, and then re-install a better design. Design is so cheap compared to redoing work that it makes good design the single most important thing you can do to save money over time, benefit the environment, and improve your quality of life.

The photos in the book were taken when I happened to be driving by something that I liked or thought would add range to this book. The lighting was never ideal and often I was driving to meet a client and couldn't get the best angle without running late. I have captured a wide range of what is going on in Marin and leave it to you - the reader- to decide for yourselves what you do and don't like.

A local small-print book like this is a labor of love that I'll continue to refine with each new printing. I like to get a book out there so it can be helping people right away and get feedback about what is most useful. I welcome your suggestions or photos you may want me to include in future editions. You may also wish to visit www.MysticalLandscapes.com for additional chapters and photos that I have not included to keep such a small edition book affordable for you.

Dane E. Rose

WALLS

Most of the stone walls I build are dry-stack, using rock from local Sonoma fields (see profile gardens at the back of the book). This stone's brown color contrasts nicely with the green of many plants. The dry-stack nature of the walls preserves the natural drainage pattern of the site and saves an extra $2-4k on drainage costs for most walls. In addition to being sustainable, Sonoma Fieldstone is three to seven times cheaper than other wall-building stone.

I keep walls under four feet when possible. Walls higher than that start to feel overbearing. In addition they need a permit and require engineers to struggle with how they can calculate the load bearing strength of a given stone when each stone is a different size.

Most walls are not retaining walls. The rocky clay Marin soil can often stay nearly vertical for decades with only minimal erosion with no wall to hold it up. But walls bring a beautiful finish to such steep slopes and do provide protection from erosion and minor slides.

What follows is a sampling of Marin walls. Pick the ones you like and show the image to your landscape supplier or contractor to get information on pricing.

1

2

3

4

5

6

7

8

9

10

11

12

13

14

15

16

17

18

19

20

21

22

23

24

25

26

27

28

29

30

31

32

33

34

35

36

37

38

39

40

41

42

43

44

45

46

47

48

49

50

51

52

53

54

55

56

57

58

59

60

61

62

63

64

65

66

67

68

69

70

71

72

73

74

75

76

77

78

WALL SOFTENING

Big unbroken walls appear unfriendly and monotonous because we experience them in relationship to our own relatively small bodies. To increase a blank wall's interest and warmth break up the single mass in some way by adding diverse elements closer to our body's size.

Ways to do this include:

- Using several colors of paint to so that one big mass of color becomes several smaller masses of color.

- Using UV protected or outdoor canvases to add interest and break up the wall (see "Condo Paridisio").

- A large tree, shrub or vine that obscures the wall.

- Adding trellises or other architectural details.

- Building with several different wall materials so that the eye sees multiple sections of wall rather than one solid mass.

If you can take an eye-sore that dominates the space and turn it into something interesting, playful and easier on the eye it's worth doing. Here are a few examples.

1

2

3

4

5

6

7

8

9

10

11

12

13

14

15

16

17

18

FENCES, GATES, & ARBORS

There are a lot of these because I see a lot of them driving around and they are more visible from the street. Aside from the appeal and cost of different designs, here are a few things to consider about fences on a logistical level:

- They will need to be 6-7' tall to keep deer out.

- Solid body stain won't flake off the way paint will on wood fences.

- Metal fences will lower long-term maintenance.

- For 10-30% more effort you can often make an ordinary fence look 100%-300% nicer.

- If you like white and low maintenance you may wish to consider Vinyl with a lifetime warranty (see "Victorian Charm" at the end of the book).

It's always a pleasure to see someone who took a little extra care in a fence and turned it into something special.

1

2

3

4

5

6

7

8

9

10

11

12

If there is a gate - or neither somewhere I'd like to make it

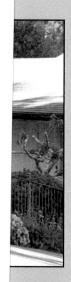

14

15

16

17

18

19

20

21

22

23

24

25

26

27

28

29

30

31

32

33

34

35

36

37

38

39

40

41

42

43

44

45

46

47

48

49

50

51

52

53

54

55

56

57

58

59

60

61

62

63

64

65

66

67

68

69

70

71

72

73

74

75

76

77

78

79

80

81

82

83

84

85

86

87

88

89

90

91

92

93

94

95

96

97

98

99

100

101

102

HEDGES

The most interesting designs balance structure and informality. An example of this might be the clean line of a nicely mown lawn with a chaos of a perennial border. Another might be a symmetrical stone wall half-covered by flowing plants that droop over the wall.

Hedges provide another way to introduce structure in a garden. Less expensive than stone or wood walls, they take time and pruning to maintain. Hedges can also be formal, semi-formal or informal. Planting a line of un-pruned evergreen shrubs would be an example of an informal hedge. How formally you prune your hedge will depend in part on your style and in part on whether the rest of the garden feels too busy and needs more order or if it feels too formal and needs more organic shapes to soften excessive structure.

These images will help you clarify what you do and don't like. Take that information to your Designer or Nursery to help you make the right plant choice for your garden.

1

2

3

4

5

6

7

8

9

10

11

12

13

14

15

16

17

18

19

20

21

22

23

24

25

26

27

28

29

30

DEER-PROOF GARDENS

Deer are a wild-card. That's because plants fall into a pecking order where deer are concerned. If roses are available for a deer's dining pleasure, they may spare your Ceanothus. If Ceanothus are available they may spare your Rhodies. If Rhodies are available they may spare your shoes. If a deer is hungry enough it will eat just about anything. And the hunger level of deer varies neighborhood by neighborhood, based on how much food is available.

It even makes a difference if your plants are tender and newly planted (yum! yum!) or tough and established (not so tasty). What I show here are examples of deer resistant plantings based on the fact that deer frequent each of the areas these photos were taken around Marin. It's worth considering deer resistant plantings for all or some of your garden because it is a lot less fuss and cost than building fences. If you do have a fence make sure it's six feet tall if you can't see through it or seven feet tall if you can. Take these pictures to a nursery or designer and have them help you identify and order the plants you like in these pictures.

7

8

9

10

11

12

13

14

15

16

17

18

19

20

21

22

23

24

25

26

27

28

29

30

GREAT MARIN PLANTS

DEER, DROUGHT AND YEAR-ROUND INTEREST

Here are some of the best plants for Marin in the current state of drought. Since I want it to be an easy list for you I've limited it to plants that have year-round interest, are cold-hardy and deer-resistant.

You should always trust your own aesthetic over any author's or designer's. No one can tell you what you should like and you will be the one looking at your garden every day. Also know that plants are on a continuum: Deer will sometimes eat anything, some are more showy than others and few plants need the exact same amount of water.

This list is intended to be used in conjunction with your landscape designer or local nursery staff. I'm a big believer in talking things through with someone who knows the plant and your situation. No list or book can account for all the many variables but The Sunset Western Garden Book is a start and you can look up these plants there or online.

In an effort to make this list even more useful I've visited local nurseries and confirmed that all of the plants are either already stocked or are available for special order through regional wholesalers. As of fall 2014 at least you can avoid that most annoying of things: Carefully researching a plant only to be told it isn't available! A few bonus plants and additional chapters are available free online at: www.mystical-landscapes.com/Images-of-Marin-Gardens.html.

Ceanothus gloriosus 'Anchor Bay'

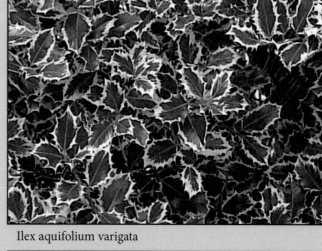

Ilex aquifolium varigata

Echeveria agavoides 'Prolifera'

Santolina chamaecyparissus

Leonotis leonurus

Passiflora 'Lavender Lady'

Cordia boissieri

Coleonema 'Sunset Gold'

Echium wildpretii

Grevillea lanigera 'Coastal Gem'

Grevillea 'Peaches and Cream'

Gravillea 'Little Honey Ball'

Cassia artemesioides

Agave 'Blue Flame'

Agave angustifilia 'Marginata'

Mahonia 'Golden Abundance'

Cerastium Tomentosum

Arbutus unedo

Cordyline 'Electric Flash'

Juniperus chinensis 'Blue Point'

Assorted 'Hen and Chick' Succulents

Miscanthus sinensis 'Variegatus'

Nandina 'Sienna Sunrise'

Cupressus sempervirens 'Glouca'

Arctostapholos 'Emerald Carpet'

Chamaerops humilis argentea

Echeveria pulv 'Oliver'

Chondropetalum tectorum Small Form

Lavendula augustifolia 'Hidcote'

Evergreen Clematis 'Avalanche'

Nepeta reichenbachiana

Lantana montevidensis 'Alba'

Miscanthus sininsis 'Adagio'

Ramnus Californica 'Leatherleaf'

Buxus microphylla japonica

Rhododendron 'Saphire'

Olea Europaea 'Little Ollie'

Elaeagnus ebbingei 'Gilt Edge'

Rosmarinus officinalis 'Irene Renzels'

Rubus Pentalobus

Variagated Lemon Thyme

Trachelospermum jasminoids

Magnolia grandiflora 'Little Gem'

Phlomis fruticosa

Teuchrium fruticans 'Azureum'

Laurapetalum 'Plum Delight'

Tulbaghia violacea 'Variegata'

Leucodendron discolor 'Pom Pom'

Salvia argentea

Carex divulsa

Fremondodendron 'California Glory'

Lavendula 'Goodwin Creek'

Teucrium Chamaedrys

Echeveria agavoides 'Prolifera'

Dasylirion longissimum

Polysticum Polyblepharum

Leucodendron 'Safari Sunset'

Podocarupus 'Icee Blue'

Liquidambar styraciflua 'Rotundiloba'

Ficus pumila

Cistus salviifolius 'Prostratus'

Agave Desmetiana 'Variegatus'

Leucadendron 'Safari Sunshine'

Hespero Yucca whipplei 'RBG'

Berberis lomarifolia

Yucca elphantipes 'Variegata'

Stachys byzantina

Westringia fruticosa 'Smokey'

Tibouchina heteromalla

Sarcococca ruscifolia

Salvia coccinea

Salvia clevelandii 'Winnifred Gilman'

Santa Rita Tubac

Phormium 'Cream Delight'

Beschorneria albiflora

Phlomis pururea

Prostanthera ovalifolia 'Variegata'

Graptosedum 'Vera Higgins'

PLANTERS AND POTS

Planters and pots heat up in the sun, making daily watering a high priority. Drips can be fed up through the bottom or taped to the back of a pot to lower maintenance and keep plants alive when travelling in summer months.

Pots are one good way to introduce edibles to a kitchen area. If you have deck near the kitchen (hopefully not accessible to deer) a few pots or planters can bring herbs, tomatoes etc. close enough that you will actually use them.

Planters are also a way to extend decks by mounting them to the outside railing and posts. This can bring color, fragrance and/or wind-protection and privacy to the deck without making it smaller. Just make sure the deck is strong enough.

High-glaze ceramic pots are a great way to bring year-round color to a landscape. They can be placed in existing beds that lack color as well as entrance patios. The scale of the pot is one of the most important aspects. For example, if your entrance ceiling is nine feet tall a three foot pot will tend to look great whereas a one foot pot may look misplaced. Here are a few samples of pots and planters in use around Marin.

1

2

3

4

5

6

7

8

9

10

11

12

13

14

15

16

17

18

19

20

21

22

23

24

25

26

27

28

29

30

TREES

Trees provide a number of important resources when appropriately used:

- They can lower air conditioning bills by keeping a house in shade, as well as lead to more time in the garden on hot days.

- They can reduce wind flow, creating a natural windscreen.

- On slopes they often help to prevent landslides.

- Aesthetically then can help make otherwise overbearing houses on smaller lots look more in scale by adding another large mass for the eye to compare the house to. Since what looks "big" or "small" is largely relative to the size of nearby objects, a big tree can help an otherwise big house look smaller.

As you look at these photos imagine what the same photo would look like without the trees. These photos are not intended as recommendations but as reference points for you to notice what you like, don't like and how you would rearrange things to suit your taste better. Take that information to your designer or nursery staff to find the right tree for your garden.

1

2

3

4

5

6

7

8

9

10

11

12

13

24

15

16

17

18

ROCKS

Rocks are low maintenance, drought tolerant, deer proof and look great when lit at night. They don't even need to be mown or pruned! That's a lot to be said for something that can be as striking next to many plants as the best companion plant.

Boulders from Sonoma are also surprisingly inexpensive and can be delivered fairly easily with machines. When placing rocks they will look more natural if they are partially buried in such a way that you can imagine a much bigger rock continuing beneath the ground.

One of the biggest mistakes people make is choosing rocks that are too small. A rock that is one foot tall and two feet wide may look great when you first plant around it. But even a lavender plant will completely cover it within 18 months. If plants are around your rocks the smallest size you want is usually three feet in diameter.

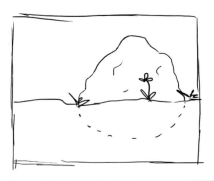

1

2

3

4

5

6

7

8

9

10

11

12

13

14

15

16

17

18

WATER FEATURES

Here is a small sampling of simple water-features I've encountered around Marin. Things to consider when installing your water feature include:

- Test for splashing. Many prefabricated fountains quickly drain and create wet areas due to splashing. A pump will burn up if water runs low. An auto-inflow valve can lower maintenance and preserve pumps.

- Moving water looks great at night lit up. You can use underwater lighting or point spots at moving water from outside the water feature.

- Shade, low nitrogen and moving water all help to control algae.

- An underground electrical box or a plant in front of an outlet on a post can help avoid the situation in picture #1 where the outlet to the right of the bench is ugly and distracts from the beautiful composition.

Custom water features usually start at around $4,000 and should include a skimmer and auto-inflow valve to lower maintenance. Prefabricated water features start at around $300. and go up from there. Sound is an amazing addition to any garden, as is moving water and light at night.

1

2

3

4

5

6

STEPS

An ideal set of steps is safe, attractive and durable. Most wood steps with ground contact get very slippery in the winter and rot out in about ten years. Railroad ties, though coated in creosote, are an exception. They are a good choice for less-expensive utilitarian areas because they are not slippery.

One of the least expensive ways to build stone steps is to use prefabricated stone or concrete risers with large flagstone treads. All unpolished stone is generally safe because it is not slippery (see "Creating a Home" at the end of the book).

When designing steps it's good to paint them out on the ground using upside-down spray paint. Before you build them imagine looking at them from different angles. Where would you want the landings? What would make them attractive to walk or look at? Six or more steps without a landing will discourage people from optional walks to explore the garden so considering this when doing your grading.

By code railings are often required if there is more than an 18" drop off the side of the steps. Grading can be done to raise the soil along the side of steps so that a railing is not necessary. This is beneficial when a railing would obscure a desired view.

1

2

3

4

5

6

7

8

9

10

11

12

13

14

15

16

17

18

PAVING

Driveways are often the first thing that I notice when arriving at a property. In some cases they dominate the view both inside and out. That makes the texture, material, shape and color of driveway paving one of the more important design choices that you will make.

When pouring new concrete keep in mind that a different finish may add only 10-30% more to the total cost but could increase the appearance by 50-300%. If you are going to go to the trouble of forming and installing new concrete you owe it to yourself to give some thought to the best shape (easy to turn around and park in), color and texture. Before tearing out a cracked concrete driveway it's worth considering re-surfacing processes that can make an existing driveway look brand new. There are also many uses for recycled broken concrete that can save you money (see "Scottish Estate in Novato").

1

2

3

4

5

6

7

8

9

10

11

12

13

14

15

16

17

18

19

20

21

22

23

24

25

26

27

28

29

30

31

32

33

34

35

36

37

38

39

40

41

42

43

44

45

46

47

48

49

50

51

52

53

54

55

56

57

58

59

60

61

62

63

64

65

66

MAILBOXES

Everything that draws our eye's attention is part of a garden's composition. Mailboxes definitely fall into that category. Here are some considerations when choosing the ideal mailbox for your garden:

- Does it bring a smile to your face?

- Is it as inconspicuous as possible (color of box and post) so it disappears?

- Does it complement the garden by integrating shared elements (for example a stone frame in the mail box that matches the stone of a nearby wall)?

- Does it have an integrated small parcel lock-box or storage area so that mail will be safe and delivery can continue when you take short trips away from home?

What follows are some of the many fun and interesting ways people take delivery of their mail across Marin.

1

2

3

4

5

6

7

8

9

10

11

12

13

14

15

16

17

18

19

20

21

22

23

24

25

26

27

28

29

30

SHEDS AND MORE

There is a great bit of building code that excludes most structures under 120 square feet from the need for building permits. Want a little office away from household noise? Or an occasional guest room that doubles as a video game hub for the teens? A variety of prefabricated structures can be purchased with different levels of comfort and polish. Other uses for structures can include a hot-tub house, sauna, garden shed, tea-room, storage shed and more.

There is a surprising level of fun stuff you can do for very little when not hemmed in by building codes. Scavenging about, some sheds can be built entirely of recycled materials.

Look at these structures as opportunities to enhance the garden aesthetic as well as your quality of life. If family friction is being caused because there is too much noise or not enough space... If you are not painting because you don't have a studio.. If you need something instant to block a particular view between you or a neighbor.. then 120 square feet of inexpensive and un-permitted space could be the biggest gift your landscape can give you.

1

2

3

4

5

6

GARAGE DOORS

It's natural for our brains to dismiss things such as "Garage Doors" when doing landscape design. This is a mistake – particularly for the good numbers of homes in which the garage door has more visual impact than the beds along the driveway because of its central location and bright white color.

It can be less expensive and more impactfull to make an adjustment in the color, texture or style of your garage door than to the planting design in neighboring beds. Next time you drive up to your house practice being in "beginners mind" and see where your eye comes to rest. If it's on a plain or ugly garage door changing it could be the easiest way to refresh your home's curb-appeal - a particular value when preparing a home for sale.

1

2

3

4

5

6

7

8

9

10

11

12

13

14

15

16

17

18

19

20

21

22

23

24

25

26

27

28

29

30

MATERIALS

This chapter has three goals:

1. Show you a few of the more important materials that are readily available.
2. Explain the pros and cons of each material.
3. Give you a rough sense of the costs (These change!).

You can do all of these things even more effectively by visiting American Soils in San Rafael, where many of these photos were taken, or other material vendors. However, for those of you wishing to make quick decisions, or who are short on time, this chapter will save you a few hours.

It's not generally a great investment to pay 100% more for a material you like only 15% more. On the other hand if a material costs 30% more and you like it twice as much, that's a great return on the additional investment. For a more thorough index of materials you can visit the "books" section of www.MysticalLandscapes.com.

Note: For an exclusive coupon giving you a 10% discount off of your first order at American Soils, buy my other book: "Successfully Landscaping Your Marin Home."

1

Black Mini Mulch. This is a dyed black wood chip. It's similar to normal micro bark (below) in function but gives you another distinct color to play with. $40. per yard.

2

Large Gorilla Hair. This is among the least attractive barks. It's benefit comes in being the only bark that will stick on very steep hills. $32. per yard.

3

Fir Bark 3/4". If you like a larger "chunk" look this is a good choice. It won't stick on hills and it won't block weeds as much as the other barks on this page. $60. per yard.

4

1/4" Playground Fiber. This is among the neatest barks. It does a great job of keeping down weeds and holding water. $46. per yard.

5

This is an irregular bluestone flagstone. It's benefit is that it will not fade. It can also be dyed fairly permanently, should you wish to bring in more color. $450. per ton.

6

Tile is great when you have an existing slab you want to cover without changing the height much. Otherwise it is more expensive than flagstone. Typically in the $2-5. per square foot range.

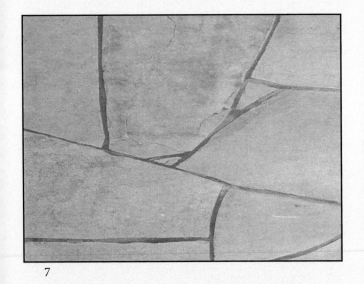

7

Arizona Flagstone is large, inexpensive, and fairly smooth. It loses it's color rapidly (note all the gray in this picture), develops mould spots, and is not very strong. $280. per ton.

8

This is one of several more colorful flagstones. It is harder than Arizona flagstone, holds it's color, and is more expensive. California Gold (shown here) is $600. per ton.

9

10

Large Sonoma Fieldstone is inexpensive at $150. per ton. Because plants fill in and obscure smaller stones, something this big, slightly buried, is ideal for most gardens.

Another variety of Sonoma Fieldstone. Once placed, rocks are zero cost and maintenance, providing grade and color contrast with bark and plants. $135. per ton.

11

12

This stone is round and smooth, making it excellent for simulating a dry river-bed, or for integrating with a water feature. $350. per ton.

Kryptonite boulders are beautiful because of their striking angles and contrasting colors. $300. per ton.

13

14

Sonoma Fieldstone's brown colors make it an ideal contrast stone with greens. It's also the least expensive stone at $130. per ton.

This goes well with bluestone but is actually called "Brownstone." It can be built with mortar for twice the cost (shown here) or using a dry stack method. $320. per ton.

15

16

This is another form of Bluestone with mixed colors. Mixed colors are cheaper than all blue, and also more interesting. Regular cuts in stone cost more than natural stone shapes because they require more labor and diamond blades. $600. per ton.

This is a mixed color natural variety of bluestone. $480. per ton.

17

18

Mexican pebbles start at this size and go up to the size in picture #2. They all cost around $480. per ton. Their uniform color and elongated shape makes them very attractive.

Mexican pebbles are often linked with a contemporary style. They can be used as a mulch, a dry-river-bed, or drainage swale. They can enhance a desert look. $480. per ton.

19

20

Salmon Bay pebbles are slightly translucent. Two good uses include lining the bottom of a water-feature, and as the last 2" of mulch in planted pots. $320. per ton.

Similar in shape to the larger Mexican pebbles, these can be used alone or in a patterned mix with the black mexican pebbles. $480. per ton.

21

22

Decomposed Granite, or "DG," makes a great pathway surface that compacts almost as hard as asphalt if installed properly. It's color goes well with the green of many plants. $95. per yard.

Blue Pathway fines is also ideal for compacted paving area. It is slightly better for a driveway than DG, because it is bigger. It's other benefit is it's cost: $55. per yard.

23

24

Small round decorative gravel does not compact well and can be unsettling to walk on. Using it to surround stepping stones is one option. $600. per ton for this American Soils blend.

This is a larger version of DG. It has a lovely Mediterranean look. It compacts less than the smaller version. $85. per yard.

25

26

Cut bluestone can be used in a variety of forms and shapes, with or without gravel, used as spacers. Most of these are around $600. per ton.

This is a 2" thick pre-cut select color Bluestone. One option is to plant between the cracks, though bare-areas often develop as you see in this photo. $650. per ton.

27

28

Broken concrete recycles waste and is typically free. This is one example of a 40 yard pile. It builds one of the strongest walls. You can see samples of this in the profile of "Scottish Estate in Novato."

Here you see the effect of mixing several types of flagstone together in a mosaic. The materials are all in the $600. per ton range. The only extra cost is labor.

GOOD IDEAS

What makes something a good idea is not it's absolute value, but rather its value relative to its cost. Think of an idea like a stock. If you could have an overpriced Google stock you would be paying a lot for a great company. On the other hand if you could buy McDonalds at a ratio to assets that would effectively mean owning their real estate portfolio for half of its quick-sale value that would be a stunning investment not because you enjoy eating at McDonalds but because you are buying it at a price that is at least 50% discounted.

That's why it's important to understand the costs of a given idea. In landscaping it's not just the value of the materials we look at, but how much enjoyment a particular idea can bring us relative to it's cost. I'm going to make a few notes under these photos to highlight what caught my eye.

As a designer what excites me is when something is done inexpensively that accomplishes multiple functional and aesthetic goals simultaneously. I'm particularly impressed when an idea turns a resource that is perceived as waste into an ideal solution to a problem. In the chapter titled "Scottish Estate in Novato" the use of broken concrete and other recycled materials illustrates this well.

1

River rock in a swale can provide low-maintenance contrast to plants and a place for storm water to seep into the ground.

2

This river rock provides a transition between a lawn and a tree that is raising the soil around it. The color contrasts with grass, bark and tree.

3

This design allowed the wall to extend to the street by an extra 2' while still maintaining access to the water meter.

4

Rather than pay $2,000 to have this giant stump removed, the client spend $400. on bird feeders that bring fun and color.

5

This bench, cut from the waste logs from a large bay tree will last much longer than most other benches and used free waste materials. It took less effort to make this bench than to haul the wood to the dump.

6

The trellis for this community dog watering spot was cut from an unwanted redwood sapling and was built in two hours. The chalkboard is used for neighbor communication.

7

Stacking pots is one way to play with plant art (naturally the plant design has room for improvement).

8

Tile shingles make a pleasing border and use waste material in this raised bed. Logs from removed trees can be used in a similar way.

9

This is a magnificent sculpture carved out of the bottom 20' of a large tree that was re-moved. It looks stunning and in some cases won't cost more than getting rid of the stump.

10

This shows the equivalent of a chain gutter. It's much more delicate and ornamental than most gutters and easier to attach.

11

Rocks can provide a great place for house numbers.

12

This community drinking fountain was in-stalled on private property for all to enjoy. It's inexpensive and a way to build community.

13

This deck railing, made with plywood, inexpensively accomplishes three things: Privacy from the street, protection from the wind and an architectural face-lift that improved the value of this rental building.

14

Here is one way to protect windows from the sun without using blinds. This means that the garden is enjoyed even while the sun is shining at the window.

15

Many Marin homes lack the level ground to accommodate play structures on one level. In this garden I put the tower on an upper level and graded the area level for a lawn to place the swings on.

16

Shaping plants is one of the least expensive and low-impact ways to introduce art into a garden.

DESIGN PRINCIPLES

Think of design not as a beautiful piece of paper but as a process that integrates your garden with your values. If lower maintenance and increasing re-sale value on your home are your two biggest values then a great design for you will insure that everything you do lowers maintenance, maximizes curb-appeal and increases appraised value. This is what makes design so personal: A good design is ultimately about you and your priorities and very little about what a designer thinks you should do.

I discuss the design process in more detail in periodic classes at the College of Marin and in my book Successfully Landscaping Your Marin Home. However, here are a few things I consider whenever making a design decision.

Minimum Effort for Maximum Result:

What's the easiest way I could achieve this particular result both in long-term cost, maintenance and hassle. Whenever you have two choices you like equally pick the less expensive one. Avoid paying a lot more for something you like just a little better. This results in a much nicer garden overall because it stops you for blowing your budget on trifles that don't justify the expense. Then when you have a really important idea that will make a big difference you have the money to spend on it.

Easy to Use and Functional to Maintain:

Every time I meet a client with a vegetable garden down long winding paths and many steps I find a client who is not tending the garden. Why? Because it's awkward to use and maintain. It wasn't set up to make it fun and easy to grab a handful of fresh parsley for the tomato sauce. And that's where this principle of design comes in. Any time you do something think about how to go about it in a way that is useful and easy to maintain.

Masses with a Human Scale:

As human beings we like things that have a human scale. Why do huge office-buildings feel cold and unfriendly? Because they are hundreds or thousands of times bigger than we are and it's hard to feel personally connected with something that is so disconnected from our own 4-6' size.

The same is true when any two objects interact. A one foot altar might look special on a small bedside table but out of place and dinky when placed in the driveway near a car. A good rule of thumb is to group objects together that are not more than three times bigger or smaller than the objects near them. In order to feel personally cozy in a space it's ideal for the objects closest to you to range from 2'-18' in diameter, which is a range of about one third to three times the height of the human body.

Scale also relates to distance. The farther away we are from something the smaller it appears, relative to our own body and the things around us. What this means is that in addition to being aware of the scale of objects to one another, we need to consider the distance from which they will be viewed. For example, the delicate shape of blue-bell flowers will be perfectly clear when planted on a pot on the deck, but viewed from one hundred feet away you might need to plant fifty times more blue-bells in order for the color blue to be briefly noticed by the casual observer.

A Balance of Integrity and Interest:

One of the reasons nature is so beautiful and peaceful to our eyes is it's simplicity. Looking at a mountain in nature we see two or three colors and textures repeated thousands of times with very small variations. By contrast, most amateur designs are a loud hodge-podge, reflecting many impulse-buys over a period of time. Often it's hard to find an overall theme because plants were selected one at a time and planted without working towards an overall composition.

While a purely native garden that integrates 100% with surrounding wildlife can be too plain and messy for many tastes, a disorganized hodge-podge is rarely as satisfying as an overall design that integrates common themes and materials throughout the landscape.

Big Picture, Little Picture:

This principle relates to the sequence you will want to design in. It's important to know what your big goals are before getting lost in the minutia. This is true around time, cost, values and enjoyment. For example, if the big picture is that you don't want to stress around money and need the project done by the time you leave on vacation, keep those clearly in mind and make sure that the smaller decisions you make are not counter-productive to these goals. In the same way, design your hardscape, pathways, parking etc. so that they are functional to use before fussing about where to place the annuals.

It's easy to get lost in the little things. The best results come when you step back, identify your core values or goals and then respect those. This is one of the most valuable aspects of an overall design: It helps you see the big picture of what everything will cost, how long it will take to do and how the garden flows and fits together as a whole. From that vantage point you can make much more informed choices on all levels.

Balance and Flow:

The most satisfying spaces leave us feeling centered. To create this experience we apply and balance the many elements in design that pull our attention. For example, sound pulls our attention and so does light. If all of our attention is being pulled forward because the light is in front of us, we can balance that by adding sound behind us - such as a fountain or outdoor speakers. Since our eyes follow lines we can create a shape with lawn, paving or otherwise that draws our eye in a direction that balances out the various pulls towards another direction. I go into this much more thoroughly in my textbook Successfully Landscaping Your Marin Home.

Intelligent Stages:

Since most of us are not in a position to do everything we want now, analyzing the best sequence to install in is important. This is where a professional can help you. You don't want to install a nice front garden only to discover that you could have saved $10k by using a large piece of equipment to grade the back yard; furthermore, now you can't get to the backyard because the machine will have to drive over all your new plantings. Installing things in the right sequence can save you 30%!

An Ounce of Prevention Vs. a Pound of Cure:

Design, research, communication and up-front negotiation all play their part in avoiding problems down the road. Preparation has more leverage to save you money and hassle than any other thing you do! Ten minutes noticing a mistake on paper may cost $20. in consultation fees but save $750. redoing that mistake later on. A conversation that clarifies working expectations may cost 20 minutes now but save weeks of unnecessary stress with your contractor. Remember that gardens are about fun, beauty and quality of life. Why not go about creating them in a way that reflects these values?

Teams Trump Stars:

Great teams in any sport out-perform bad teams with great stars. The same is true in your landscape collaboration. An OK landscaper who makes a real effort to show up and partner with a client who does not have any expertise in gardening but who also makes an effort will often have better results than a top landscape company who has a client that is too dis-organized to partner well on the project.

For a great team experience wait until you have the time and energy to enjoy participating in the decisions so that you get what you want. Similarly, look for a landscaper who is interested in being on your team in the ways that are important to you. These might include them working certain hours or it might include you having your infant take a nap in a different room rather than asking the crew to stop noisy work at 2pm while still hoping the job will be done on time. In all cases, discussing these details before the contract is signed insures that your agreements will match your expectations.

GARDEN PROFILES

NUTS AND BOLTS OF TRANSFORMING GARDENS

In this section I'll present ten dramatically different gardens that I designed and installed in Marin, along with practical information that will help you decide whether or not the ideas are good fit for your home. Each garden is different in both style and function because each of the people I designed them for had different preferences, values, and locations.

I make an effort to discuss costs, neighbors, permits and couple-dynamics because these are left out of every garden book I've seen but have much more impact on you and your quality of life than the color or variety of a perennial.

CONDO PARIDISIO

IT BEGAN WITH A PAINTING...

The first call I got from this client was a question about fees. Would I be willing to do a $450 project? Since I don't have any policies about budget other than that it has to be enough to do what the client wants, I said, "Sure."

When I got there the number had changed. "What would you do for $5k?" We spent an hour of design time looking at how to improve his little condo garden. I told him that I would have fixed bids for each of my ideas when we met again. On the third meeting he surprised me again: "If you had $15k to do whatever you wanted, what would you do?"

I got into a more serious design mode. The more that is being spent, the more profitable and important it is to look at a project from multiple angles. I felt the first thing was to get to know this client more fully. The garden's sole function was to be a source of joy for a retired bachelor who enjoyed hosting friends from around the world. I decided to start with his art collection.

Touring the house, I noticed the brightly painted walls and the pride he took in showing me his European impressionist paintings. Then it struck me. His favorite painting was of a garden about the size of his condo garden! If he liked the painting so much, surely he'd like having an actual garden like that even more. I felt that what would make it truly original was transferring the bold impressionist colors into what was currently a drab, gray condo garden.

The trick was to do all this without violating

condo regulations. The association owned the exterior of the building and so nothing could be altered that would affect the external appearance of the garden as visible from the street. Fortunately, there was a 6' wall around the garden so I suggested that we go to town below that six foot wall and create a hidden oasis of color.

It was a lot of fun! I brought in the umbrella concept in part because it was a way to sneak above the 6' limit without raising too many eyebrows. Just as importantly, the umbrellas made the garden more enjoyable in the San Rafael heat. There was one umbrella in particular that I felt passionate about for practical reasons. The client had a screen nailed over the outside of the main sliding glass door that overlooked the garden. The purpose of this was to protect the dining room table from fading and block out the intense afternoon sun. But this screen also blocked the view of the garden from the key window. Unless I could find another way to block the sun the client would be spending a lot of money to improve a garden he would not see.

I thought that an 11' offset umbrella out at the edge of the property in direct line with the sun would solve much of the problem. I found one with a tilting mechanism that turned the umbrella into a vertical sun-sail. It worked!

I also tackled the issue of reducing sun-light on the table another way: There were some openings in the architecture that currently let light in. I thought the place to start would be to insert stained glass for both shade and light protection. I had some colored Plexiglas cut to the exact size and tacked it into place so that it could be easily removed in the event that the client moved or anyone objected in the association.

Next came the idea of wall-mounted umbrellas with colorful fabrics that would overlap to create a unified shade canopy. In such a small garden wall-mounted seemed key: the large bases on most umbrellas would make the space feel crowded and act as trip hazards. I found a custom manufacturer in China who could make and ship these for $600. each. I was also excited because the umbrellas made the space twice as functional and attractive (the garden would be used in the sun) while costing only 10% of the budget.

The client didn't have the heart to tear out the gray Trex deck he had recently paid $8k to have installed. I didn't like the color or the way it made the space feel boxy and smaller. Trex is not easy to paint. I decided to experiment and turned the situation around by finding vivid enamel colors that tied in with the painting and have held up over time.

When I came across an 18th century antique door frame I thought it would fit right in to his favorite paintings. We went from first tacking it up on the wall as an empty frame to buying outdoor vinyl art to insert inside the frame to make it appear that we were looking through a doorway into a European garden. Since the garden art was not big enough to fill the whole door frame, I suggested building a faux gate to deepen the illusion. I also liked the fact that this illusion made a small garden look bigger. As an added bonus, the roses in this picture never got

black spots, stopped blooming, or needed pruning! (See main photo of this garden.)

We had a lot of fun with the tile, though the online company we ordered them from shipped them a month late, to everyone's annoyance. Most of my jobs are done early and I prefer to keep control of my materials, etc., so that work can be done on time.

The result of this project has been that friends of the client from around the world have wanted to visit him to see the garden. I decided to use this garden for the cover of the 2014 edition of *Successfully Landscaping your Marin*

Home.

This garden ended up costing $25k. The client was clear that this was his fun money and we both had a lot of fun brainstorming all the ways we could play in such a small space. I appreciate this client for the chance to express this side of my creativity. I begin every design by listening to each client and designing in the way I think will most please them. What made this client different was that he was open to experimenting and playing around. The result is a one-of-a-kind garden in my 22 year portfolio. Thanks, David.

CREATING A HOME

...AND IMPROVING RESALE VALUE

When I began the design process for this client the wife wanted to either have more than a hillside of weeds or move. The husband, whose focus was on investing, was more interested in increasing rent on a vacation rental that was part of the property and improving resale value. Since the poor quality of the landscape was the biggest depressing factor in both rental income and resale value I was able to help both of them get what they wanted.

We spent three months and $150k transforming the property with several objectives:

- Create a level lawn.

- Create pathways and steps that made the steep slopes accessible.

- Stay within $150k.

- Create a garden shed for tools

- Create a dog run with dogs that liked to sit on and destroy plants.

- Increase real estate value.

- Create an attractive private garden for the rental unit that would allow them to charge an extra $300. per month in rent. This in turn would pay the 2nd mortgage payment and generate positive cash flow for the whole project.

There was an old orchard on the site that we all liked. The problem was that it had been planted on a steep slope and as we created a level area for the lawn, it would mean that some trees were too high and others were too low. So I came up with the idea of raised beds around some trees and sunken beds around others. The sunken beds required drainage at the bottom so that the fruit tree roots would not rot or hold water. While I've never seen this done before, it's worked out great over the past 10 years and the trees have thrived (see sketch below).

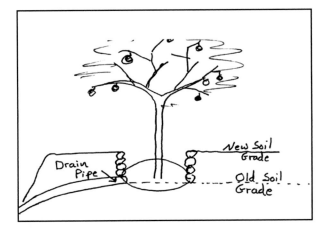

It's always a bit tricky learning what the deer will eat in a given neighborhood, but we did all right. In the back, we raised the existing fence in one section and put in a gate so that it is deer-proof. We created the dog area by partitioning an area. This gave the dog free rain from the back door through about 1/3rd of the garden and the fence was not ugly to look at.

There was some talk about fencing the property in for deer, but I suggested sticking to deer resistant plants for the front garden to save $20-40k in fencing and automatic gate costs. I also wanted to avoid the hassle and eyesore of a gate to let cars in and out.

We did a lot of grading on the property to make it functional to use. This is where my experience with heavy equipment came in handy. I would grade a given area for steps, walkways, walls, and a patio and then get out of the machine and walk about in the space to see how it would feel as a user in the garden. How would it feel to sit in this patio? Would the walls feel comfortable to look at and sit beside?

This is my favorite way to design. This particular client left me largely to my own devices, providing I stayed on budget. A lot of design refinements don't affect cost but do affect the way an area feels. I like being both a designer and installer because it is my weeks on the job installing that help me understand all the different aspects of a site and allow me to refine my ideas as I execute them.

This house had a shallow, low-producing well so we connected it to the irrigation system in twenty minute cycles to save a considerable amount on the water bill. More of my clients are weighing the costs of drilling a well as water-shortages increase.

CONTEMPORARY WARMTH

INSTANT PRIVACY FROM NEIGHBORS

The job began with a call asking for a bid. When I asked the client if he had a design, he said "No. The site has so many limitations there is not much I can do with it. I don't want to waste money on a design when the solution is obvious." This is a sentiment that leads many people to feel that design is a waste of money. Why indeed should anyone pay money to be told to do the obvious?

The reason for this perception is that the ideas we can't imagine appear nonexistent, creating a state of blissful ignorance of better ideas we can't see. A key value a good designer brings is the ability to show you possibilities you cannot currently see.

I suggested that it would be highly beneficial to have me review his ideas before spending tens of thousands installing them when there might well be ideas he would like much better than his current plan.

About 50% of clients in this situation say, "No." They don't want to pay me to review their ideas or create a design. This is the end of the relationship for me. I want to work with clients that understand how much they don't know because only then will I be able to easily share my expertise and help them by putting it to good use. I've spent twenty years developing the ability to spot areas of unnecessary waste, problems with maintenance and comfortable living, as well as ways to improve a home's resale value and aesthetic appeal. I consider it to be my most valuable asset along with my willingness to take a design all the way through the installation process on time and on budget.

This client was one of the 50% in a call like this that said, "Yes." We met at his house the next day after work and he showed me what he had in mind.

I saw immediately that he had not considered any of the ideas that would really change the site for the better. He loved the ideas I suggested so much that he asked me to come back again for another meeting to refine them and go over costs.

The first thing that struck me in the front was the lack of privacy or space for a seating area in the sun. The tiny back yard was narrow and shaded while the front was a steep slope all the way to the street. I imagined a sunken patio that would (by sinking it) create a large enough level area to sit but would also give it more privacy, helped by the concept of a ring of 3'-4' plants between the patio and the street.

This one idea transformed the front and dou-

bled the amount the garden was used.

In the back area, my most important idea was to lower the existing concrete wall (see first photo of this profile). In the full-page photo, you can see that the backdrop of the water-feature is

18" taller than the rest of the wall. That's the only area of the wall that remains at its original height. I lowered the rest of the wall and removed four dump-truck loads of soil from behind it in order to create a low enough planter and wall that it

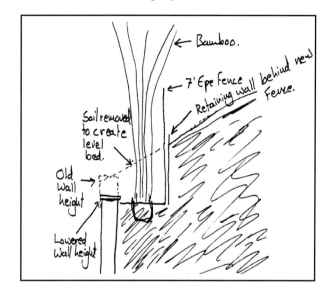

could be enjoyed from the house windows.

Having level area dramatically increases the sense of space, which I thought was important in such a cramped back garden on a hill. When the grading was complete, I built a retaining wall to hold back the remaining uphill slope and then faced that with a seven foot Ipe fence.

When I began, the neighbors could look directly into his windows from their deck. The goal was to create a 12' screen of some kind to interrupt this line of site. Bamboo came to mind because it can be purchased that high almost instantly, but it also does not grow any higher. Unlike other trees which grow a steady 1-3' per year and keep on growing, bamboo comes in certain height ranges that are rapid but stable. In addition, it fit in with the more contemporary style that the homeowner wanted for the back garden.

This was also the perfect site for bamboo. With a concrete retaining wall in front and a 4' retaining wall in the back it, would be naturally contained within the bed. This would save us the cost of putting in bamboo barrier, which would normally have added $3k to the project.

When I had begun the project, the client stressed his modest salary and an absolute maximum budget of $54k. Since this was a tight budget for the scope of work I gave him a $54k design and cost-breakdown. For me it's important to stay within an agreed budget since I don't think gardens – intended for relaxation – should be turned into a source of stress by spending more than one can afford.

The client then proceeded to request an additional $40k for work in bits and pieces as the project progressed. One week it was adding lighting. Another it was the water feature for the kitchen view. The ideas were all good and the garden came out fantastic.

However, I've noticed that the best designs come when all the money is organized as a whole up front with as few changes to the job as possible as it continues. I wondered if perhaps he had just assumed I would try and up-sell him and had held money back so that I could "persuade" him to spend more money. I know some contractors make their money this way, but I don't think it's ideal for either side. The best way is to work as real partners and stick to whatever is agreed.

This project turned out very well for my client financially. He sold the property less than a year after the landscaping and netted a considerable net profit for his two years of home ownership. I met the new owners who love the house and garden. One of them has a horticultural degree and the garden was an important part of their buying decision.

EXPANDING A SMALL HOUSE

ECHOING ARCHITECTURAL DETAILS

My first mandate from this client was to re-do the driveway in the picture below. In a situation like this the driveway surface dominates the view regardless of what else is going on. For this reason I prefer to turn what is essentially a functional eye-sore into the most beautiful part of the landscape. I do this by treating it as a work of art rather than a utility surface. On this job we used stamped concrete with a high gloss finish in colors that complimented the house.

You can also see the importance of painting the garage door, adding windows and echoing the house-colors in the fence.

I decided to focus on integrating the deck outside the front door with the living room. My strategy was to borrow colors, materials and shapes inside the house and bring them outside so that the transition between house and landscape was less noticeable.

This garden is at the base of Mt. Tam. and often gets cold fog blowing through, making eating on the outdoor table uncomfortable. A wind-break (see lower right page) in glass block seemed like a great idea for three reasons:

1) Using glass blocks would integrate the deck space with the inside of the house, where glass blocks had also been used.

2) The glass block partition would not only serve as a wind-screen, but help create the feeling of an outdoor room.

3) The wood frame provided another way to extend the architectural details into the landscape by using the house paint color on the frame and matching the design of the eaves.

Half-way through the job the client mentioned that they were going to throw out their existing BBQ unit to get something more fancy to go with the new landscape. I thought it was

My second mandate was to take a small house footprint and make it feel bigger by making the outdoor space more usable. The goal was to blur the boundaries between the house and the garden so that more of daily living would take place in the beauty of the garden. There are health and financial benefits to this approach as outdoor renovations cost 80% less than interior renovations and it leads to spending more time outdoors.

a shame to throw out something that worked very well and could not imagine the new stainless steel unit looking much better. The new unit would cost several thousand dollars so I suggested that we get creative and spend that money achieving several goals:

- A fireplace to provide some heat for the cold foggy nights.

- Bring the look of the living room fireplace out onto the deck by using the same stone (see next page).

- Increase the wind-block by making a wider solid mass than a typical BBQ.

- Mask the new BBQ with a stone veneer which is more attractive than stainless steel.

- Recycle the existing BBQ and spend about the same price as buying a new BBQ.

The end result was a stone-encased BBQ that doubled as a fireplace, with a chimney and spark arrester. The gas makes starting fires easy and stainless steel lids keep in the heat when cooking food. Because the stone facing was too heavy for the deck I drilled three sonotubes through the deck into the ground below. This design means that the deck can be repaired or re-built in the future without affecting the BBQ.

In one of our conversations the clients mentioned that they disliked their roof line and were considering spending $30-50k to make it more interesting from the street. While I agreed that their existing roof looked plain, I saw several downsides to a major roof renovation that I explained to them:

1) In a small house with nowhere to go, they would upset their lives for many months with the redo of their roof.

2) $30-50k also seemed like a lot of money to improve appearances. I suggested we consider less-expensive approaches.

3) Dealing with city permits and all the arcane regulations drives many people crazy. I suspected that by the time they were done with permits their lives would be much worse off than doing nothing at all and having an old-fashioned roof line.

A great idea in my eyes would make the roof more interesting, integrate home and landscape, avoid the need for building permits, be less expensive, and avoid damaging the roof.

The idea I came up with was to bring the fence trellis theme onto the existing flat roof by pouring what were effectively 3" thick concrete snow-shoes in which I placed 2' fence posts. These were heavy enough to hold the trellis in place but not directly connected to the roof. They looked a little bold initially but as they have

grown in with vines they have become quite lovely. The loveliest part was the price, however. Rather than $30-50k we installed these for $7k, no disruption to the client's life and no permits!

The ideas that excite me are those that, like this one, lower the cost by three to eight times while only lowering the value 50%. This is how good design pays for itself.

The final technique that we used to expand

the house was to install a small garden shed, painted to match the house. Since the profile of a shed greatly affects the way a space feels, I always encourage some thought when choosing a shed. Kits are often the way to go, as seen with this shed. However, the right kit is one that will

add allure as well as functionally to the space.

A few years later I met the buyer of this property, who bought it largely for the landscape. I also met a potential buyer who didn't buy it because he thought it was too expensive per square foot. My client was able to increase the perceived value of their home significantly by using landscaping at a lower price per square foot to increase the quality of life overall for anyone who lived there. The person who didn't buy it was quite happy as well: They bought an ugly house with many stairs that was cheap per square foot. This is why knowing our values is key to our design.

PROTECTING THE VIEW

PREPARING FOR A SALE

Anyone with a great view has probably paid a lot of money for it. In some cases, the view will double or triple the value of a home. This amounts to hundreds of thousands of dollars – even millions.

The project you see here had a nice view of Mount Tam and parts of the bay. My primary mandate was to prepare the property for sale but do it in a way that was pleasing to the owners – just in case they decided to stay. The budget was $50k and our starting point was about 2,500 square feet of old uneven bricks set in sand, with weeds growing through them.

I have a couple of thoughts about view properties:

- If you are going to pay hundreds of thousands more for a view, then the view should give you more pleasure and satisfaction than the landscape you could build for hundreds of thousands of dollars.

- If you have spent this kind of money on a view, the landscape should not steal the show with a colorful foreground. It's always easier for the foreground to outshine the background; the way to get the most out of a view is to create a serene and simple foreground that allows the eye to travel easily out and enjoy the view, un-distracted.

I put an ad on Craig's list for people with a large truck and a big crew to have as many bricks as they wanted for free. A pickup truck and solo operator were going to take weeks to transport so many bricks so I specified the kind of manpower and vehicle that would get them out of the area rapidly. This is key when I've done stuff like this on Craig's List.

Lawn and play area is at a premium in Mill Valley and the home seemed suitable for a family that might buy it just for the large area of level lawn to play in. Lawn is also one of the cheapest types of landscaping to install per square foot. But trumping all of these things is that it is serene and simple: the perfect foreground to allow one's eyes to enjoy the view.

I recycled a few of the bricks we tore up and re-laid them in a herring bone pattern with dry mortar brushed between and an inch of dry mortar underneath. I like this approach because it is half the cost of mortaring the bricks on a poured concrete slab but has most of the benefits of slab and mortar in both stability and weed control.

We put mole mesh under the grass since we knew moles were a problem. Amazingly, the moles were so active that they would pop up around the irrigation sprinklers in the lawn where we made holes in the mesh for the sprinkler heads to poke through! I used sonic mole-chasers and did some extra patching around the heads before we finally won the war with the moles.

We used Mexican pebbles instead of bark in the flower beds for several reasons:

- It added a contemporary feel to the prop -erty.

- The clients were passionate about keeping wood and subsequent termites away from the house.

- The wind picked up on the mountain and the client was concerned about bark blowing around in a storm.

We also built a small Ipe half-fence (see below). The height was chosen for being just tall enough to block the view of the street from most areas in the garden, while not being tall enough to block the view. My client liked the garden so much that after putting the home on the market and buying another house, they decided to move back and sell the home they had just bought!

FINE-TUNING A MASTERPIECE

INTRODUCING CRYSTALS

I was called out to this property to help with a very narrow scope of work: satisfy the Mill Valley fire department. Brush needed to be cleared. 3' weeds needed to be pulled and cut. The dry meadow needed to be mowed. I don't normally do maintenance, but when I arrived, I saw the bones of one of the nicer properties I've come across. I wanted to see the property restored. So I took the job.

My client was a young man with a lot on his mind, so the normal design approach wouldn't work. Rather, I found that he liked to make one decision at a time and spend around $15k per 6 months doing something that was easy to think about. Over several years following this approach, I was able to restore the garden to its original glory and add a few embellishments, such as the lighted agate stepping stones below.

It was a real pleasure to see a home and garden that truly impressed me. I learned that an architect had built the home for his parents and the love and attention to detail really showed. That being said, it was very neglected. Moles had destroyed the lawn. It had not been pruned in years and there were so many weeds that it was impossible to see all the amazing specimens.

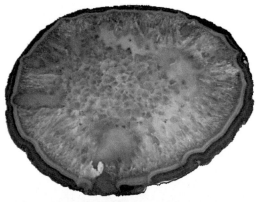

When the client decided to sell the property, I borrowed experience from my days as a General Contractor on Whidbey Island and saw that the inside was restored as well, refinishing all the floors, putting new carpet down, painting, cleaning the windows, and many smaller jobs. I knew that if I didn't take the initiative, these things would not get done with such an absent-minded client and the realtor was grateful for my help. We both knew that the house could not get top dollar in its present condition.

Aside from the restoration, the work I did on the property included:

- Adding a bocce ball court on a slope by first building a new retaining wall.

- Building a half-circular patio inset in the lawn outside the pool room.

- Planting a new hedge at the edge of the lawn to create a clear transition from for-mal garden to informal slope.

- Seeking and obtaining a Tier-4 exemption permit to lower water-bills that were as high as $2,000. per cycle before the exemption.

- .• Adding an on-site weather station to control the extensive irrigation.

- Setting up the garage as a workshop including custom shelving.

- Building a shade arbor to protect the pool equipment from UV rays.

- Installing a crystal fountain.

- Installing lighted agate stepping stones on the front walk.

- Adjusting some of the planting areas.

- A new concrete walkway and a sunning patio near the refurbished vegetable garden.

When making adjustments to a well-designed property, one of the most important things is not to dilute the design by introducing too many new elements. When I added a gate to keep the client's dogs in part of the garden, I was careful to match the existing style and paint of the perimeter fence. It turned out that the metal fence was painted using a Porsche car paint, which led me to learn how Porsches are painted and to do the most extensive paint preparation for a fence in my career. One of the finest aspects of this house was the way that the inside extended naturally to the outside. For all of its five acres of land and majesty, it was only a 3 bedroom house.

It had a separate pool building that was covered in vines when I arrived and proved quite a challenge to restore while working over a swimming pool. One thing I love about fine design is that it is worth restoring and preserving. It would have taken just as much work to restore a poor design, but this house and landscape was fun to bring back because it was so carefully and tastefully thought-out to begin with.

The crystal fountain was my personal favorite part of this project. Crystals are 40-200 million years old and each one is a total original. Then there is the fact that they look even more beautiful at night when lit up and bring year-round-interest to a garden. Add to that the fact that they are drought-tolerant, deer resistant and don't need weeding and it's amazing there are not more people integrating them into their

gardens.

I found an amazing Brazilian quartz point weighing one hundred and twelve pounds and I thought it was stunning. I designed a sketch for my client with a three rivers flagstone base and showed him what it would look like in the vanishing pool that was already there. Threading low voltage wire through existing conduit so that it could all be lit up at night made such a difference.

Then there was the question of what to do with the large planters on the tiled patio. The client would never water them and they had no irrigation. I decided that the best thing would be to create art with crystals and crystal tumbles to tie into the water feature. These would not require any water or maintenance. Xeriscaping is a

form of design that eliminates all need for water. Arranging rocks in beautiful paintings of color and texture is a great xeriscaping technique.

SCOTTISH ESTATE IN NOVATO

THRIFT IS GOOD.

My client on this project is a Scotsman. He grew up on a large estate, was comfortable operating farm machinery, and wanted a project that would keep him busy for a few years. He loved a deal, and appreciated every one of my money-saving ideas.

As I took all this in, I was reminded of how different each of my clients are. It's one of the reasons I begin each design process by asking clients to fill out the extensive landscape questionnaire. It's job is to help me see a client clearly enough that my suggestions will reflect their values and not my own.

My client was too thrifty to hire me for design initially so we met when he attended one of my classes at the College of

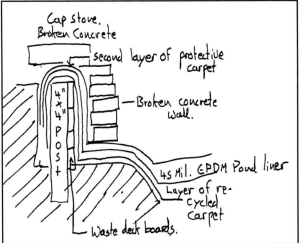

Cap Stove.
Broken Concrete

second layer of protective carpet

Broken concrete wall.

4" x 4" Post

45 Mil. EPDM Pond liner

Layer of recycled carpet

Waste deck boards.

Marin. When his garden was randomly drawn from the hat as the sample garden that I and students would practice design in, we all spent four hours looking at the best way to respond to his situation.

He had a large property – several acres. He also had neighbors who were loud sometimes, prompting the idea of introducing a source of white noise that would allow him to be on the deck without hearing them. A water feature came to mind. But knowing his thrift, I first suggested something less expensive: "What about a Bose system with speakers and a water track on an endless loop? It's no maintenance and much cheaper and would provide you with all the white noise you wanted?"

The single most important idea I had was buying my client a piece of heavy equipment for the job. I knew that without heavy equipment, he would never be able to transform his acreage. This meant either contracting out for it to be done for around $60k or buying a used machine for $30k and teaching my client to use it.

I worked out that if he bought the machine for $30k, used it for two years, and then sold it, he could get the full $30k back or at most take a $10k hit and save a minimum of $50k on contracted equipment. This was an exciting idea. And given his experience with farm equipment

as a child, I felt confident he could learn to operate it. I had taught myself how to use this same equipment early in my career when doing land development on Whidbey Island: an 045 Takeuchi excavator with a blade and thumb.

I negotiated and purchased the machine on my client's behalf, giving him a few lessons. Having just seen how one idea had saved him $50k, my client was convinced that hiring me as a consultant was the thriftiest thing he could do. So he did.

There were several things that tipped the scale towards what would ultimately be the biggest water feature I have installed. The idea of a 70' water feature was a response to several different values that all came together:

and perhaps going paddling with his kids.

- The house was on a hill and the garden seemed unapproachable. I thought that making a fun destination in what was currently the low spot of the property would lead to the garden being used more.

- The pond would reduce the size of the lawn and (once filled) require less water than watering a lawn. This would save money on the water bill.

- A large pond of this type is lower maintenance than any other type of garden. You don't have to mow, water, or weed it.

- With the machine, my client would be able to construct the entire pond for around $15k in materials. Meanwhile, having the pond would add about $70k to the property value, create a reservoir to use in droughts or in case of fire, and add something unique to the property.

- A fountain would provide the white noise between client and neighbor property.

- Client enjoyed the idea of fishing in a pond

- The water would remind the client of Eu-

ropean gardens as an added bonus.

With all this in favor, it made the pond a no-brainer. Accessing free fill-soil that I helped the client locate, he arranged to have about one hundred dump truck loads of material brought on site to serve as a dam for the valley, turning a gully into the shape of a large pond. The next step was to get carpet companies to bring by their carpet scheduled for the dump so that the liner could be padded. We bought a very large 45 mil EPDM liner that would cover the whole pond without any seams in the liner. This meant that the liner weighed close to two tons, and so I used the machine to take the liner from the truck and delivering it to the pond site.

I supervised the pond liner installation because the cost of a mistake was so high (a tear leading to a leak would be very hard to find and repair) if things went wrong. The broken concrete we used to line the pond and build all the retaining walls with was another idea I gave the client to save money. He loved the look which reminded him of Scottish castles. Even more, he loved the fact the idea saved him $20k in stone material costs. He was able to do the entire proj-

ect for around $70k, including some expensive wire mesh under all the extensive lawn to prevent mole damage. The 100 yards of wood chips needed were delivered as waste chips from local arborists at no charge.

The client paid me $10k to consult and walk him through this process with some help on the machine at times. This allowed a project that normally would have cost $140k to be done for half that. The property will have appreciated by between $220-450k due to landscape enhancements when it is all done. The front, which is not complete yet, includes re-routing the driveway and adding an automatic gate to make the whole

property deer proof. The client is making six figures while able to spend time with his kids and enjoy gardening. Good for him!

My reward? After demonstrating on the machine that an access road could easily be built from one area of the property to another I received the honor of having it officially referred to as "Dane's Lane." I've requested that a proper sign be put up but the same thrift that leads to flattering me instead of hiring me to install the garden is no doubt at work conserving sign materials. I live in hope that one day Alistair will spend the $10. to buy a board so that the lane named after me can have an official sign! Perhaps I'll give out his e-mail in the next edition so you can all lobby him on my behalf.

HOME OF AN ARCHITECT

It's always fun to work with other designers. I did this project for an architect and his wife, who both took an active interest. Here were the goals:

- Budget of $70k with some discussion of doing it in stages.

- Improve the appearance of the steep ivy and weed covered slopes that abutted the street.

- Connect a pathway to an existing set of steps that currently went nowhere.

- Generally increase its beauty.

- Create privacy in the back garden along with an area devoid of deer.

- Improve the way cars passed on the narrow street in front of the house.

- Remove an old deck that blocked the view and replace it with something more permanent and attractive to look at through the house windows.

While there was some initial interest on the part of the client to use wood retaining walls, I pointed out that, inevitably, wood ends up looking like the walls we were here to replace. Even at their best, wood retaining walls rarely look as attractive as stone a few years after installation. But stone can be a lot more expensive if it is mortared in place. Additionally, mortared walls require extensive drainage behind the wall to reduce the pressure of water build-up.

My suggestion was to use local dry-stack fieldstone. It's about the same cost as wood, lasts forever, is more sustainable (in that it does not require dead trees) and does not require drainage (water drips out of the cracks between the rocks rather than building up in any one location).

Given that the slope behind the walls was so steep and I wanted to do the base of the wall at the edge of the drainage ditch to the side of the road, I was concerned that the wall might collapse in a storm if run-off eroded the soil under the wall's base. Of even more concern was my

awareness that the county would periodically clean out the drainage ditch using heavy equipment. Sloppy operation would no doubt result the backhoe bucket hitting the wall and causing a failure. Finally, the existing ditch was a traffic hazard. It was so sudden that cars trying to pass could get stuck if they drove even slightly off the road. This made it difficult for cars to pass. I was also bothered by the idea that the foreground to the new walls would be tall weeds growing in a messy ditch.

I wanted to do something inexpensive that would solve all these problems at once. My answer came in the form of lining the ditch with

4-8" of dyed concrete. I reasoned that if this was done right, it would save the county money in maintaining the ditch while at the same time making it unnecessary to clean out with heavy equipment. I loved this idea because, for $2k, I would be achieving all my goals simultaneously:

- Keeping the county's machinery away from my walls.

- Blocking the messy weeds in front of the wall permanently.

- Creating a more gradual transition so that cars could drive off the road into the gut -ter to pass without getting stuck.

- Eliminating soil erosion under the wall.

- By pouring the concrete right up and around the first layer of stone it would become part of the walls structure and add

even more stability than a concrete footing that would have cost more than the gutter and not achieved as much.

- By dyeing the concrete to match the color of the stone it would add to the curb appeal rather than take away.

Next came the installation strategy. Technically, we were supposed to get a permit for blocking the street. But this would have thrown a monkey wrench into the whole plan. The county might ask for engineering which could easily cost more than the entire installation. They would require flaggers, signs and barricades that would also cost more than the entire $2k price of installation. It was important to come up with an approach that would not stop such a good idea from happening.

This is one of my most important roles as a project manager: seeing that bureaucracy does not stop a great idea for all concerned from happening by driving up the cost to a point where the client doesn't want to do it. It's always a shame seeing our government spending taxpayer money to slow down and raise costs of ideas that benefit everyone on the street because of some technicality.

Our way around the permit process was not to block traffic at all. By carefully preparing the ditch area by hand, we did not interrupt the flow of traffic. We then prepped our cement truck driver on a way to deliver the concrete without stopping. He would slowly drive by the property at about 1 mph while someone walked behind the truck, directing the concrete from the shoot into the ditch. My crew used shovels and trowels to smooth it into a smooth and attractive gutter that would allow water to flow, support the wall, and hold up under the weight of cars.

In ten minutes, the concrete company came and left, leaving us with a few more hours of work to do by hand. We never stopped a single car in the process and the whole neighborhood benefited due to the fact that we were able to come up with a way to keep costs to a level where the idea was doable.

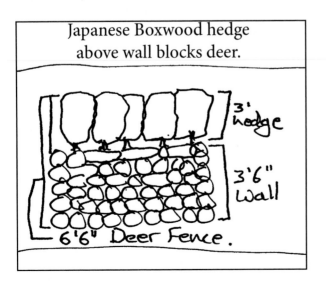

Japanese Boxwood hedge above wall blocks deer.

3' hedge

3'6" Wall

6'6" Deer Fence.

Another innovation on this project was an inventive deer fence. The view from the upper terrace we created was spectacular and we didn't want to mess it up with a 6-7' fence. I came up with the idea of transplanting an existing boxwood hedge immediately on top of the 3'6" wall I was creating to expand the amount of level space in the back garden. There were just enough 3' hedge plants already on the site to run along the entire section of new wall. This would create a 6'6" vertical face that a deer would have to jump up, even though from the top, the hedge was only 3'6" tall. This would not only save money and re-use existing hedge plants, but would maintain the view (see sketch to left).

The technique we used for the new stairway was to curve steps built into the hillside up the slope in an organic shape. This technique, which uses concrete prefabricated risers and irregular flagstone, is the most cost-effective approach I know for creating attractive stone steps. In addition, I love the fact that the stone I use is much safer than wood when wet. Most wood steps develop a layer of algae in winter that can be treacherous to walk on.

I like stone patios because they are much lower maintenance than wood decks and don't distract the eyes with the visual clutter that comes from introducing so many rectangular shapes above the ground. I suggested that we replace the two-tiered deck with a two-tiered flagstone patio, replacing the square deck with natural curves. This turned out well. I used a high quality stone that holds its color called "Three Rivers" flagstone. It is called "Three Rivers" because it is quarried in a location where three rivers converge, each bringing unique mineral sediment and color. As a result it is one of the most colorful stones available, containing browns, purples, reds and oranges, which look beautiful next to most plants.

We did the project on time and on budget for our $70k, and I had one lesson in neighborly etiquette along the way. I had ordered a very large load of chicken manure shipped straight from the farm to save money on soil amending. It cut the client's cost by around $400 to have it transported in this way rather than on several small trucks from local soil suppliers. But this meant that we had a big pile in the driveway for a week as we distributed it to all the beds for soil amending.

The plants loved it, but all the neighbors had a great time holding their noses every time they saw my client or commenting about the fresh air in loud voices over the fence. I often order grape seed compost these days from the regional wineries because it also has a high nitrogen content without the smell of chicken manure. The only other feature of note on this job was how much fun the client and I had driving radio-controlled cars around the job site. Gardens projects should be fun when possible.

VERTICAL GARDEN

IMPROVING A MILL VALLEY DRIVEWAY

While our work on this property was more extensive, the story I tell here centers around the challenge of deciding how to improve a difficult driveway. After taking my class at the College of Marin, the client approached me to give them a price on extending a poured concrete wall along the driveway. The concrete concept was going to be expensive ($30-70k) and would require permits and engineering. The bigger issue was that because the driveway was so narrow I didn't think a wall right next to it would make drivers feel more comfortable than the existing ivy. When you are driving an expensive car a few inches away from a narrow concrete wall many people feel uneasy.

My first suggestion was to remove the ivy, grade the slope a little, and plant a hedge of Nandina (heavenly bamboo) at the bottom. This would be more attractive than the wall, harmless to cars, and deer-resistant. The client liked this idea. Because Nandina it is a slow-growing plant, the plan was to bring in about seventy plants that were already 4' tall, bringing the installed cost to around $18k.

Then the client brought up their interest in vertical gardens. Their thought was to put a vertical garden on a bare piece of concrete on the house. Aesthetically this was a great idea. However, using the prefabricated vertical garden sections they had found which cost $100 per 3' section and another several hundred to plant each one it would be very expensive per square foot. It got me thinking that we could make a more extensive and useful vertical garden on the

newly graded driveway slope for much less per square foot.

My goal was to save the client money by getting rid of the prefabricated sections of vertical garden at $100 each and use the rocky slope itself as a material to chip out planting holes in the rock. With that in mind, I gave a fixed price that included:

- Grading and removing 40 yards of rock and ivy to soften the driveway slope: $10k. We capped it at 40 yards because anything more would have triggered a grading permit with Mill Valley which, in turn, would have triggered engineering reports that would have tripled the cost and the hassle. As long as we are improving the safety and stability of what has been there for more than 50 years, I prefer to avoid engineers who are required to recommend costly upgrades to get insurance. I used the machine I had bought for my Scottish client (see "Scottish Estate in Novato) to do the grading.

- Buying and planting 700 4" plants for the cliff face and irrigating them: $12k. This reflected the fact that planting would occur on a cliff and that each planting hole would be chipped out of fractious rock.

If all went well, we would have a dramatically enhanced slope with a softer vertical garden for about half the cost of the original concrete wall. The client would get a bigger vertical garden and cars would not be driving close to a hard wall. But, while I had given a flat cost to do this project, it was not at all clear that things would go as planned. About 5% of what I do are things I have never seen done before so I need to make educated guesses and make contingency plans.

When the grading was done, I tested the slope to see how our plan of digging holes in the rock face would work. Tying a climbing rope to the deck posts, we descended with crowbars and hammer drills to the slope face and did a few test holes. The vibrations from making the holes created little slides as surrounding rock broke free; it was clear that this approach would not work.

I had four contingency plans in place, knowing that nothing about this project would be predictable. I ended up needing all four of them. My fourth contingency plan was to use galvanized fencing as an armature that was anchored at the top of the slope using 3-5' metal stakes and nylon cables. To this I stapled pressure-treated 2'x4's to create a backdrop to which I could staple polyester fabric, which I then painted so we would not have to look at the ugly gray color until plants filled in. Polyester was important because it is UV resistant and tough. Fortunately, I could get 300' rolls of it at a reasonable price.

If I had used the prefabricated vertical garden sections the client had researched just the infrastructure would have cost $20k. I was not happy about the fact that in the prefab design, the soil pockets were only about 4" in diameter.

This seemed like a poor long-term fit for plants. Anyone who has tried to sustain house plants in 4" pots for very long knows that the plants get root bound and stressed because there is not much stored fertilizer in such a small pocket of soil. The custom planter pockets I built gave at least 1' of soil per plant.

The client and I agreed to do three vertical sections of hanging gardens in rectangles and then plant creeping figs in between. This was partly a compromise between the couple. One member liked the creeping figs more and one liked the vertical garden more. It worked. The planters that you see here are less expensive than the prefabricated models on the market while giving plants much more soil to grow in. Attached to a galvanized armature of fencing, they also add a stabilizing weight that discourages slides and stops stray rocks from falling down in those areas. The whole thing was possible without permits and for less money than a less attractive wall. As the creeping figs fill in the whole surface will become a living green wall. The photo below was done right after install.

VICTORIAN CHARM

NEVERLAND FOR MOM

This garden was commissioned for an elderly mother by her daughter. The goal: give the mother a magical place to hang out in for her last years of good health. The daughter's primary value was to do things right the first time and never have to replace or repair things.

The pictures shown to me by the client in the design stage were in a style that I call Victorian Cottage Charm: white picket fences, beautiful flowers, and a little whimsical. I was initially asked what I thought about the idea of transposing something perfectly symmetrical into the space. However, the space was irregular and to maximize it meant creating an asymmetrical path layout. I suggested that what would look

best were winding paths and curves that were functional, with an organic shape.

We visited local material suppliers and settled on bluestone as the daughters favorite material. Initially, we thought to do the pathway in bluestone tumbled pavers. However, since the goal was to use a $30k budget, I suggested DG as a firm and much less expensive alternative. Although initially rejected, when the bid came in at $19k for the tumbled bluestone on all paths and resurfacing a concrete patio, the bluestone became a stage two option. Since DG is a great base for pavers, the bluestone can always be added later on top of the DG.

The focus on never replacing or repairing things led to Vinyl for the fence and Gazebo, both with a lifetime warranty. This was a learning curve for me as it always is when dealing with a new material and supplier. In this case, I would be dealing with one supplier for the vinyl fence and another for the vinyl gazebo.

I had initially thought to build a spacious and fairly simple custom wood arbor over a sitting area for around $4k. But when I found a vinyl kit for the gazebo you see in this garden, I suggested it as being better value at $6k because of how it fit the theme and because it could provide covered seating for dinners in the garden.

We decided to make it into a lit outdoor eating area with a hanging light fixture that matched fixtures in the main house that we retrofitted to operate on the low-voltage light circuit.

We used a lot of light fixtures for such a small garden – around 36 in total. The daughter designs kitchens and brought that attention to detail to the idea of having lots of fixtures and creating small pockets of light.

The project came in at $45k. It's quite magical. The only drawback that I see is that the mother we created the garden for seems to be afraid of messing up the design when the point of the garden was to give her a nice space in which to fiddle. This as a danger whenever we make things too perfect: it can stop feeling comfortable to live in and the emphasis can shift to the object rather than to enjoying ourselves and our lives in our home. When I built a community dog-oasis for neighbors, I used all recycled materials and down played the workmanship so that everyone on the street would feel comfortable helping me build it and using it.

Let's all join together to banish the days of living rooms filled with plastic-covered furniture that no one can sit on! (Note, I heard from the daughter that Mom is now feeling more comfortable being herself and gardening.)

Mystical Landscapes

HOW CAN WE HELP?

Clients sometimes ask me: "Dane, I only have a small project. What's your minimum project size?" While our average project is $50k, I don't think about project size. My focus is on the quality of thought that goes into the work and the quality of my relationship with the client. I prefer a $600. project that is an ideal fit for that client and location than a $100k project that will need to be redone in a few years because the design was rushed.

This is why I see Design as the most important element of the project. It may take as little as ten hours to do a great design. But just one of those hours might save you 100 hours of maintenance over the next ten years, with thoughtful plant choices. Another of those hours might insure that you can turn your car around easily, avoiding a $5k ding to your Mercedes. Another hour might add $20k to your resale value by helping you maximize curb appeal. Design is the one activity in the process with the highest return on investment. It's why I encourage you to find the best designer you can, be that me or someone else.

Once I sign a contract with a client I give full-attention to one job at a time until complete. As both your designer and installer I am able to provide easy and accountable communication as your sole-contact point with Mystical Landscapes. By giving you flat costs for all installation it means that you can relax, knowing that the cost will never go up unless you make a new request.

ABOUT THE AUTHOR

Dane Rose is the owner of Mystical Landscapes, a design and installation company formed in 1992. His interest in gardening began at age ten on an organic Estate in Sussex, England, when the gardener taught him pruning and compost-making.

Keen to do work sensitive to the environment, he chose landscaping as his career at age seventeen. After seven years as a landscape designer/installer he obtained his general contracting license in Washington State and built several custom homes with the goal of offering informed input to clients in areas where home and landscape design intersect. Over the years he has taught more than fifty classes on landscaping and design at community colleges in Washington State and Marin.

MARIN LANDSCAPE DESIGN